Don't V

for the

Wake up Call!!!

By

James Robinson

Eli Press
121, Low Etherley, Bishop Auckland, Co. Durham DL14 0HA

2011

First Edition 2011

© Eli Press

ISBN-978-0-00000-000-0

Printed by

Eli Press
121, Low Etherley, Bishop Auckland,
Co. Durham DL14 0HA

I dedicate this book to:-

Pastor Richard Gibson
Moyra Gibson
Phillip Gibson

and the late Andrew Gibson.

On many occasions when I have been in the caves of deep depression through problems in my own life I have travelled to see Pastor Richard who first introduced me to Jesus many years ago.

I always came away feeling as though the weight had been taken away from me as we prayed together.

Pastor Richard and Moyra have endured great suffering in their lives after losing a beloved disabled son Andrew at the age of seventeen. Richard also contracted Parkinson's disease.

It humbles and inspires me when I hear them. Praise our beloved Jesus Christ our Lord and Saviour. I realise even through the trials and tribulations in their lives their faith has gotten stronger.

May God bless and keep them safe.

Acknowledgements

First of all I give thanks to the Almighty God for His inspiration in writing this book.

Extracts from the Authorised Version of the Bible (The King James Bible) the rights of which are vested in the crown are reproduced by permission of the crown's Patentee, Cambridge University Press.

I would like to thank my daughter and son in law Rick and Nicola Cotto for their guidance along the pathway to Jesus. Sincere thanks to my brother Thomas William Robinson for his © wonderful poems and words of wisdom. Thanks to the very Rev. John Ervine the Dean of Coventry and his P.A. Sharon Crofts for allowing me to use 'The Coventry Litany of Reconciliation' © of Coventry Cathedral.

I could not have completed this book without the perseverance and calmness of my nephew George Robinson – sincere thanks.

I would like to thank Wear Valley Christian Centre for inspiration.

I have tried to source anonymous and unknown material.

Any material that may sound similar to any other material is purely coincidental.

I have tried my utmost to give acknowledgments to all texts that are not mine.

And finally to anyone I may have missed especially the writers of Christian Literature that have inspired and helped motivate me towards my redeemer Jesus Christ.

Praise be to GOD!!!

This is an enlightening book
about what steps you have to take in order to get to
your Eternal Redeemer
and the only way
to get the pass you require
to get into Heaven.

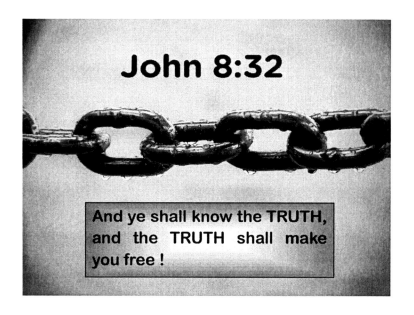

Therefore if the son makes you free
you shall be free indeed – John 8:36

Insight into The Triune

God gave me sight to illustrate The Triune to
explain in a simple method for all to grasp.
Father, Son and Holy Spirit.

Each member of The Triune has a
Christian purpose.
God the Father is the Creator.
Jesus the son is the Redeemer.
The Holy Spirit is the sanctifier.
A simple method of illustrating this is to take an
apple and squeeze the juice out of it.
What do you get?
You get the goodness of the apple.
If you do the same with an orange you get the
goodness of the orange.
If you do the same to a pineapple you get the
goodness of the pineapple.

Each one is the goodness of the fruit.
Each one can quench your thirst individually.
If you mix all three together you get the
goodness of all three together as one.
It is the same with God.

We should all thirst for goodness.

Let

God the Creator

God the Redeemer

God the Sanctifier

Quench all of our thirsts with His goodness

One in All, All in One

Praise be to God!

The Door

I stand at the doorway ready to call
All who will hear me into my hall
The Kingdom of Heaven is opening wide
To meet with the love of my chosen bride
The promise I made at the
beginning of time
Is written in the book
the book that is mine
Let the wisdom and knowledge flow through all
of your days
Till you know all my secrets
and all of my ways
One day you'll know of all of my grace
As you see me in Heaven
at last face to face .

(by James Robinson
from the Land of the Prince Bishop's)

Calvary Cross

Adam and Eve why did you deceive
Jehovah who made you to love
No sin was within till you listened to him
To the one who distorted the truth
Then you did hide on the day that you died
From the radiance of God's pure love
Were you both blind at the fall of mankind
Or did you both not understand
That the knowledge you gained
Would forever be stained
And would be troubles and earthly loss
And one day thy God would send us his son
To pay on the Calvary cross.

(by James Robinson
from the Land of the Prince Bishop's)

'I am the Way

I am the Truth

I am the Life

No man comes to the Father

but through me'

These are the words of Jesus Christ.

The only way to the chamber of God.

I've written this book to try and show all who read it the way, the only way to get the pass card into heaven and eternal salvation.

Jesus said:

'I am the way
I am the truth
I am the life'

HE IS THE GOOD SHEPHERD.

As you read this book you will notice that I have repeated certain points over and over again. This is to try and get you to realise that these points are needed and will help you get through the gates of Heaven.

Mam

We have to stop and wonder
Why life comes to an end
The grief that we all suffer
When we lose our closest friend
mother was the kingpin
She kept us all in check
She made the food
She clothed us all
She taught us all respect
So many children in the house
So many mouths to feed
Mother catered for us all
She met our every need
She never asked for anything
That wasn't mothers way
God is good and we'll get by
That's what our Mam would say

She worked so hard
Out in the fields
Providing for us all
And Mam was there to catch us
Should any of us fall
Mam was proud of all of us
Each and every one
The world seems such a lonely place
Now that our Mam has gone.

In Loving Memory of Our Wonderful Mother
Florence Robinson nee Dugdale

(By Thomas William Robinson)

Dunblanes Angels

A classroom with an open door
Where childrens voices call no more
A place where only God could give
The ones inside the right to live
Innocent every one
Slaughtered by a madman's gun
I clasp my hands I ask God why
You chose to let those children die
Heavens not the only place
Where angels tread in splendid grace
Are they now at Gods right hand
Tell me let me understand
Our souls are filled with so much pain
For all the angels from Dunblane.

(By Thomas William Robinson)

(In memory of the deceased)

Diana

You brightened the darkness
You lifted the gloom
You were a rose picked in full bloom
You outshone the stars and
You never knew why
with a beautiful mischievous glint
in your eye.
To the young, the old, the sick and infirm
You gave your love and
Your love was returned
You never distinguished by colour of skin
You held their hands and
The pride burned within
On a pedestal we placed our princess up high
The brightest light in all of the sky
Your like again will never be seen
On Earth a princess
In Heaven a Queen.

(By Thomas William Robinson)

In memory of Princess Diana

17

The Commandments

The rules and moral standards set to live a Christ like life, may God grant you peace and Love and Joy in your hearts.

God spoke
'I am the Lord your God'

1. And God spake all these words, saying,

2. I am the LORD thy God, which have brought thee out of the land of Egypt, out of the house of bondage.

3. Thou shalt have no other gods before me.

4. Thou shalt not make unto thee any graven image, or any likeness of any thing that is in heaven above, or that is in the earth beneath, or that is in the water under the earth.

5. Thou shalt not bow down thyself to them, nor serve them: for I the LORD thy God am a jealous God, visiting the iniquity of the fathers upon the children unto the third and fourth generation of them that hate me;

6. And shewing mercy unto thousands of them that love me, and keep my commandments.

7. Thou shalt not take the name of the LORD thy God in vain; for the LORD will not hold him guiltless that taketh his name in vain.

8. Remember the sabbath day, to keep it holy.

9. Six days shalt thou labour, and do all thy work:

10. But the seventh day is the Sabbath of the LORD thy God: in it thou shalt not do any work, thou, nor thy son, nor thy daughter, thy manservant, nor thy maidservant, nor thy cattle, nor thy stranger that is within thy gates:

11. For in six days the LORD made heaven and earth, the sea, and all that in them is, and rested the seventh day: wherefore the LORD blessed the sabbath day, and hallowed it.

12. Honour thy father and thy mother: that thy days may be long upon the land which the LORD thy God giveth thee.

13 Thou shalt not kill.

14. Thou shalt not commit adultery.

15 Thou shalt not steal.

16. Thou shalt not bear false witness against thy neighbour.

17. Thou shalt not covet thy neighbour's house, thou shalt not covet thy neighbour's wife, nor his manservant, nor his maidservant, nor his ox, nor his ass, nor any thing that is thy neighbour's.

Found in Exodus 20: 1-17

If you continue to reject Jesus as your saviour and dismiss him he will withdraw from your presence.

ICHABOD: The Glory is departed. (1 *Samuel 4-21*)

Jesus said the greatest commandment is:

1. Love your God with all your heart and with all your soul and with all your mind.

The second commandment also states:

2. Love your neighbour as yourself.

All the laws of the prophets are based on these two commandments.

(Mathew 22:36-40)

1. Ask ye the Lord. *(Zec 10: 1)*
2. Ask and it shall be given to you. *(Mat 7:7)*
3. Ask in Faith. *(James 1:6)*
4. Ask what I shall give thee. *(1 Kings 3:5)*
5. Ask diligently. *(Deut 13:14)*

When in troubled times – focus your attentions on Jesus.

See how he takes away your worry.

I read somewhere 'no matter where you go even into dreadful places and no matter what you see or encounter on your journey God was there before you came and will be there after you have gone.'

Praise be to God!

Jesus Said

'I am the way

I am the truth

I am the Life

No man comes to the Father

but through me'

Jesus Said

'I am the way

I am the truth

I am the Life

No man comes to the Father

but through me'

Jesus Said

'I am the way

I am the truth

I am the Life

No man comes to the Father

but through me'

(John 14:6)

I cannot spell it out more plainly.
He wants you to seek him before the
wake-up call comes.

I have repeated the words of Jesus three times because this is the way to your Eternal salvation, Eternal happiness, Eternal love for Eternity and beyond.

BUT

You have to do your homework and study to get to know this wonderful person that gave his life and suffered incredible pain and suffering. He was flailed, whipped, scorned and half beaten to death before he was nailed onto a cross.

He died for **our** sins.

I hang my head in shame for human kind. This all happened over two thousand years ago and the human race has learned very little because they would do it all over again.

If you believe and accept Jesus as your saviour
say this prayer and it will change
your inner being.

A prayer;

Father God – I believe Jesus Christ is your son
and the saviour of the world.
I believe he died on the cross for me and bore all
of my sins.
He went to Hell in my place and triumphed
over death and the grave.
I believe Jesus was resurrected from the dead and
is now seated at God's right hand.
I need you Jesus, forgive my sins, save me, come
and dwell inside me
I want to be born again for eternal salvation.

There will be a change.

I want you now to believe Jesus is living in your heart.
You are forgiven and made righteous and when Jesus comes you will go to heaven.
You have to open the door of your heart to let him come in and change your inner being.

As we travel through this life Lord
In all our troubles and pain
Keep us searching for thy love
Again, Again and again
Never let us cease this task
Till we see you face to face
All we have to do is ask
To receive thy love and grace

(by James Robinson
from the Land of the Prince Bishop's)

I will be with you as I was with Moses
I will not leave you or desert you.

(Joshua 1:5)

To be a Christian

To have a personal relationship with Christ.
To have 24 / 7 communication line to God.
The calls are free. Make that call now.
The heavenly hotline to Jesus.
To acknowledge and believe Jesus Christ died for our sins.
To acknowledge and believe Jesus Christ was crucified, died and resurrected from the dead.
 He took the sins of the world upon himself and defeated Satan over evil.
To accept Jesus Christ as your saviour for eternal salvation.
To walk constantly in God's direction.
To have the inner peace, love, joy and calmness of Jesus in your heart. To praise and give thanks to Him.
To have the baptism of water.
To have the baptism of the Holy Spirit
To repent and resist all sinfulness.
To love one another.
To love honour and obey His commands.
To be a servant to mankind.
To seek His wisdom (It will be given).

To knock at His door (It will be opened).
To ask (It will be given).
To have faith in Him.
Do not doubt or you will do without.
Focus all your attention on Him constantly, not
only in times of trouble.
He heals broken hearts.
Talk to Him like your friend.
Bear fruits for Him.
Feast on His word in the Bible.
Get to know His goodness and mercy.
Let His goodness and mercy shine through you.
Jesus is God and became human.
We are human and have to become like Christ.
To love Him and give thanks to His Holy name
Jesus is the Alpha and the Omega
 (the beginning and the end).
The positive over the negative
The light over the darkness.
The good over evil.
The life over death.
You must grasp the reality of your creator (God).
Look around you, you cannot mistake His
creations everywhere you look. Everywhere you
go, everything you see belongs to Him.
He is the provider.

His name is Jehovah – Jireh and He made it all for us.

Praise and worship His Holy name.

When you reject Jesus you cut off the power supply that illuminates the countenance of God.

Believe in the coming of Jesus Christ.

Do not judge until you have looked at all the evidence.

Become like a forensic pastor, searching for the truth.

It will set you free.

As you search and read about Jesus you will find it the most rewarding endeavour you have ever undertaken or experienced. As He reveals himself as you search He will explode into your heart. Your heart will melt and flow like a river of pure love.

The Book of Jeremiah 33 verse 3 – read what it says about the call you need to make to God's hotline.

'Call to me and I will answer and tell you great and unsearchable things you do not know'

When you have made that call to God

'Don't try to control the message you want to see or hear'.

There is a saying 'you are so heavenly minded that you are no earthly good'. The problem arises when people become too earthly minded to be no Heavenly good.

Jesus is the same today as He was before time and will be the same tomorrow – He does not change. Scientists who give their theories constantly change their opinions as circumstances in their equations change. God is not a theory or an equation.

He is a reality – A living God.

Praise be to his Holy name.

The Treasure

Look in the Book
Where the treasure map's found
Only by seeking
Will he ever astound
When you have found Him
Don't let Him go
Love Him sincerely
Let the world know
Give Him the glory
And all of your praise
And pray that He's with you
All of your days
Seek ye the treasure
Look for His field
And He'll always protect you
With His Godly shield.

(by James Robinson
from the Land of the Prince Bishop's)

'Take me as I am Lord'

Take me as I am Lord
Unworthy and I know
Cleanse me from the inside
Let your spirit flow
Your spirit is the power
That melts the heart of stone
Only you can give it Lord
Only you alone
Now my heart is open
As you have turned the key
I know you paid the price Lord
And you did it all for me
Fill me full of love Lord
Cleanse me from within
I think you always knew Lord
That you were going to win
Now my journey's over
My shepherd and my lamb
Take me up to Heaven Lord
Take me as I am.

(by James Robinson
from the Land of the Prince Bishop's)

Give Thanks

Don't let dark clouds of the past
Change your future its going fast
The time is now its time to live
Just keep remembering to forgive
Laugh in the good times
Cry in the sad
Just thank God for all that we've had.

(by James Robinson
from the Land of the Prince Bishop's)

Thy Shrine

And is it night?
Are they thine eyes that shine?
Are we here alone?
May I come near to you?
May I but touch thy shrine?

(Anonymous)

Jesus in your Heart

When your heart is wounded
And all you've done is care
Jesus is the healer
And will always be in there.

He never leaves when you're in pain
He steps in to ease the strain
When He appears He'll let you know
He's here to set your heart aglow.

(by James Robinson
from the Land of the Prince Bishop's)

True Love

Just by a loving glance
Sends my heart into a trance
It starts to melt like April snow
God is in there and I know.
He lets me know day by day
His love will never fade away.

(by James Robinson
from the Land of the Prince Bishop's)

Just Enough Lord

Never leave me weary
Never leave me dry
Never leave me grieving
with teardrops in my eyes.

Never leave me lonely
Never leave me sad
Never leave me sorrow
Or things that can be bad

I know I have to suffer
I only hope and pray
God only gives me just enough
to see me through the day.

(by James Robinson
from the Land of the Prince Bishop's)

God Knows

As I lie in this quiet place
I long to see thy radiant face
I once walked towards thy radiant light
In the tunnel of love one dreamy night
You stopped me as I moved your way
You let me live another day
I'll never forget that molten light
As You had me in your glorious sight
Now I know the God above
Who sent me home to the ones I love
Now I know the reasons why
You didn't want to see my children cry.

(by James Robinson
from the Land of the Prince Bishop's)

My Family

To all my family who I love
God sent you all from up above
I feel I want to give my all
So none of you ever have to fall
Proud of each and all of you
Give thanks to God's love pure and true
You'll always be within my heart
So be joyful when we have to part
I know Ill always be in yours
Rejoice when God lets me through those doors
No more worries, no more stressed
Up in heaven with all the blessed.

I hope?

*(by James Robinson
from the Land of the Prince Bishop's)*

May Jesus be with each of you through life.
May His love shine through all of you.
God bless you all.

Bed Time

When I lay me down to sleep
I try to always ask the Lord to keep
Me safe and sound from any harm
And soothe me with His loving balm
To guide me through my dreams untold
til morning light as it unfolds
My troubles to take and cast away
To guide me safely through the day
til one day when I fall asleep
Into thy loving arms to keep.

(by James Robinson
from the Land of the Prince Bishop's)

DIVINE SERVICE

We need to search for the divine. Experience the divine. Then with every willing act, perform the divine. Through Jesus Christ.

God's mercy is like two escalators to Heaven. As one goes up with our requests and prayers; the other descends with all our needs with what God wants us to have.

I read somewhere that Mother Teresa spoke
these words about love.

Spread love everywhere you go
First of all in your own home
Give love to your children,
To a wife or husband,
To a next door neighbour
walk a mile in her shoes.
Let no-one ever come to you without leaving
better or happier
Kindness in your face
Kindness in your eyes
Kindness in your smile
Kindness in your warm greeting Kindness
flowing from your heart.

Sometimes in the midst of weakness
we can become strong through Jesus
Out of Unhappiness
we can become happy through Jesus
Out of hate
we can become to love through Jesus
Out of being unforgiving
we can learn to forgive through Jesus
Out of darkness can come light
through Jesus
Out of death
can come eternal life through Jesus
Out of war
can came peace through Jesus
Out of sorrow
can come joy through Jesus.
Jesus said 'I am the way'

Big multi-national companies are getting rich by preying on the weak and vulnerable in society. They do this so they can pay big shares and dividends to their share holders. This is also true with the banking systems.

But the eyes of the Lord are everywhere watching the good and the evil so the Lord knows you by either the good or bad that dwells within your heart and by the fruits of your life.

This means;

'What have you done for the good shepherd?'
'What have you done to save souls?'
'What have you done to get to know the gatekeeper - the door-man who is in charge of whether you're in or out?'

Remember these words what Jesus said
'Depart from me, I do not know you'.
'If you want to know him read what he wants
you to know in the Bible'?

Open up my ear and mind
Let your words and wisdom flow
When we meet at Heaven's gate
My heart will be aglow.
When I hear your lovely voice
My heart and soul they will rejoice
Your beauty there for us to see
and it is for eternity

(by James Robinson
from the Land of the Prince Bishop's)

A good tree produces good fruit.

In other words a good person helps the needy, thinks and cares for other people and does not look for any reward. He is always available to anyone who has needs, is a servant to Christ. He maintains constant peace and joy in his heart because that's what God is. God knows you by the fruits you produce for him.

Don't live in a church that operates in its own four walls praying and not producing.

Sometimes when I talk to people about Jesus I hear them say 'I am a good person, I haven't done anyone any harm'.

I say to them 'Do you know Jesus'. I ask 'when they see suffering do they feel any pain in their hearts'. Jesus feels this pain for all of us and that **means** *All OF US*.

What a burden he had to bear for our sins.

It is by your own efforts in searching out God that gives you the reward of finding the salvation of Jesus Christ. You can't rely on the efforts of someone else to obtain this glory, it is by your efforts alone that gets you into the presence of God. In other words the response of Jesus Christ revealing himself to you is equal to your desire to want to find him. The greater the effort the greater the reward.

God is in charge of quality control through the heavenly gates.

Anyone who has done something wrong in their lives or have been unjust to someone needs to repent and ask God to forgive them. Don't try to make yourselves purer than you are. Accept the guilt that goes with the sins you have committed and repent. Don't try to transfer your guilt onto someone else to make yourself look better than you should be in other people's eyes.

In other words - Don't pull someone else down to build yourselves up.

Money can buy what you class as the good life but it can't buy the class of eternal life, only Jesus Christ can do that.

Money has never helped anyone into heaven, only by helping others in distributing your wealth among the needy has accomplished this.

God has given Man the ability to look beyond and use his imagination to look at the reality of eternal life through Jesus Christ. No other species has had this privilege bestowed on them.

Praise God!!!

'Truly my soul waits in silence for God only; from him is my salvation'.

(Psalm 62:1)

A driving instructor friend once told me 'Always teach your pupils to expect the unexpected when driving'.

I think this could also apply to us in order for us not to become to complacent. Expect The Unexpected.

God can allow your life to change in the blink of an eye. If God wants your attention He will get it.

If God wants you on your knees in front of him it will happen.

'Amazing grace how sweet the sound
That saved a wretch like me
I once was lost but now I'm found
Was blind but now I see'

(From the song - Amazing Grace)

Don't let your possessions become your possessor

When you share you care

God is love

God is peace

God is joy

God is contentment

God is fulfillment

God is satisfaction

God is relief

Sin cannot co-exist alongside any of these.

Thy Quiet Voice

Once I heard thy still quiet voice
The words you spoke I had no choice
I didn't want to hear what you told me then
Because my flesh was weaker when

You exposed me to my sinful way
for which I give you thanks today
I pray you speak to me again
You saved me from a future pain

As I try my life to unravel
Down Gods way I want to travel
I know this world I cannot trust
You've shown me all about the lust

The devil that devours people's lives
He cannot win no matter how he tries
On the cross that day he showed the good
He beat him with his precious blood

(by James Robinson
from the Land of the Prince Bishop's)

Faith

God is there don't you doubt it
If you do you'll do without it
Trust in God and he'll replace
Your sin your hate and all disgrace

Let him fill you full of love
It only comes from God above
Once you've tasted love divine
Your whole life will start to shine

As you feel him in your heart
He's given you a brand new start
As you travel along life's roads
Jesus in your heart explodes

This feeling I just can't explain
Just let it flow like heavenly rain
Now I know thy still quiet voice
Be there always and I'll rejoice

*(by James Robinson
from the Land of the Prince Bishop's)*

Neither is there salvation in any other, for
there is none other name under Heaven given
among men whereby we must be saved.

(Acts 4:12)

Commit your life and ways to Jesus Christ.

When you are feeling depressed or lonely as though nobody cares remember that He loves you. He has always loved you and it causes Him great pain to see you suffer. He wants to support you. He wants you to experience the love, peace and joy He has for you. He wants you to experience the interaction between you and Him.

When you are in the caves of deep depression turn to Him. Love Him, trust Him and He will take you to the pinnacle of the most overwhelming joy.

Neither has the eye seen nor the ear heard, nor has it entered into the heart of man what God has in store for those who love HIM.

(1 Corinthians 2:9)

There is a way which seemeth right unto a man but the ends thereof are the ways of death.

(Proverbs 14:12)

Imagine

Imagine you've found gold
Or riches untold
Or met an angel today
What would you say?

Would you thank Jesus
Who died on the cross
I think you would agree
He died not only for you
But also for me.

(by James Robinson
from the Land of the Prince Bishop's)

Make the pilgrimage of your life
towards Jesus.

I often hear people say:

'Why does God cause or let us suffer pain'.
I want you to remember that God knows all
about pain. God wasn't exempt from pain. He
allowed his only son to be nailed onto a cross for
our sins.

I once read somewhere that Hell begins the day
God grants and shows you a Vision of your life.

What could you have done?

What you should have done?

What you would have done?

But did NOT do.

Remember that God knows you by your fruits.

Do you know Him? What have you done for Him? Remember what He did for you. I am the way.

I am the truth. I am the Life. Nobody goes to the Father except through me.

I keep repeating the words of Jesus. I am the way. I am the truth. I am the life. Nobody goes to the Father except through me. He is the good shepherd. His flock will know his voice and follow him to eternal salvation.

So it is not what you have done in your life or how good you feel about how good you have been. If you don't know Jesus or have accepted him as your saviour – Remember what he said to people that thought they knew him?

'Get away from me, I don't know you'.

To all the unbelievers the name of whom you will cry out to in times of distress.

God help me
He will

Jesus Christ be with me
He is

My God
Always has been

Good God
Eternally

Jesus
The way

Jesus Christ
The truth

Abba
The life

So

Do you really know Jesus?

Do you know where he was born?

Do you know how he was conceived?

Do you know how old he was when he started his ministry?

Do you know about his miracles?

Do you know about his disciples?

Do you know about his parables?

Do you know about his love for you?

Do you know about his works?

Do you know about his healing powers?

Do you know about him being tempted by Satan and his reply?

Do you know about the people around Jesus and his friends?

Do you know how he was betrayed and by whom?

Do you know about his trial?

Do you know who turned against him?

Do you know how he was tortured and how he was made to suffer before he was crucified?

Do you know how he rose from the dead?

Do you know that when he rose to Heaven, who he sent to Earth?

Do you know about his revelations?

Do you know when you accept Jesus as your saviour, who then dwells within you?

Do you know about Faith and that when you trust in God – Don't doubt or you will do without?

Do you know about what the prophets said
about him?

Do you know what makes a difference to him?

What makes a difference is the fruits you
produce for Him. The good works you can do for
humanity and for your redeemer.
Remember
When you produce for Jesus you are letting Jesus
live through you.

REMEMBER these words

*I am the good shepherd; my flock will know me
and follow me when I call.*

Pray to God in the storms of your life.

What is true love?

Anyone who asks about true love should think about God. He knew what true love 'Does' and still 'Does'. He loved us so much that He gave us his son who gave his life to save us from hell. That's what true love is.

When you care more for the people you love and their well being more than your own.
Try not to be overcome by your own feelings of inadequacy for trying to make a difference and don't be discouraged.

Always try to help or try to make things possible and not impossible.

Remember the Kingdom of Heaven can grow from a mustard seed.

Discover what kind of involvement God is asking from us.

Get into the God squad before you get the wake-up call.

Every morning you wake-up – pray to God.

'Lord let me be a blessing for someone today .

Lord let me bring Glory to your name.

Lord let me accomplish your ways'

Lost in a daydream

I was never lost in a daydream
Though people accused me of such
I was trying to reach my ambition
But there was not a soul I could trust
Through The years of struggle and Hardship
I sought my fortune and fame
But the roll of the dice was against me
And all that I did was in vain.
As I climbed each rung of the ladder
Even when I reached the top
There was always someone there waiting
who was trying to knock me back off
But I was always a winner
With a great belief in myself
I just picked myself up and shook myself off
And climbed back up on the shelf.
How do you measure your fortune
Is it the wealth that you own
To me its the family around you
And all of the love that I've known.

(By Thomas William Robinson)

I ask people about Jesus. I keep hearing people say 'but this' and 'but that' and they try and put obstacles in the way of getting to know Him. I realise that when Jesus said *they have ears but they cannot hear'* that it is because they are not listening or do not want to hear.

'They have eyes but they do not see' or will not look for the answers. They seem to want to go through life without any direction. Them being tossed about on stormy seas like a rudderless ship until eventually they run aground and founder on the rocks being broken up. Then when is suits them or they cannot cope they cry out to God. God is always there. He would rather you look for him and talk to him when things are calm and peaceful as well as when it is stormy and turbulent in your life.

Jesus said:

'Love one another as I have loved you'.

In the last days people who believe before the wake-up call comes will be ridiculed and mocked as we are warned in 2 Peter 3:3

'Knowing this first, that there shall come in the last days scoffers, walking after their own lusts.'

'Watch therefore, for ye know neither the day nor the hour wherein the son of man cometh.'

(Mathew 25:13)

'He that is not with me is against me and he that gathereth not with me scattereth abroad.'

(Mathew 12:30)

Seek Him

Don't leave the search for him to late
Or you will never go through the heavenly gate
Seek him while he may be found
For that's where true love abounds.

Heavenly angels are preparing the way
To greet you on that glorious day
Where hearts, spirit and soul combine
To meet thy God thy creator divine.

(by James Robinson
from the Land of the Prince Bishop's)

Sometimes when we look at other people we often find ourselves judging the other person and assuming certain things about them. It is human nature to judge.

We judge them against ourselves.
It seems we want to be better, have more possessions, better qualified or to think we are superior to them.

Think Again!

Try and look at them as one of Gods creations, equal to each and every member of Gods World.

That is what is wonderful about our planet.
We are all different individuals.
Think of that famous song
by Louis Armstrong

'What a wonderful world.'

Thank God for it.

Know that the Bible has standards of living a Godly, happy life the way it was meant to be. It tells you the way God wants you to live. To live the life he created for you. To love, serve and obey him.

Delight yourself in his ways and he will give you the desires of your heart.

(Psalm 37 v3:4)

When you accept Jesus as your saviour your inner being will change. The Holy Spirit dwells in your heart and your sins have been paid for.

Once you realise this you must repent all of your sins that you have committed and resist sin. You will have to do this until the day you die because sin is in our genes passed down from generation since the fall of man in the Garden of Eden from Adam and Eve. We have all sinned and fallen short of God's grace.

When we go before God to give an account of our lives we are all going for mercy.

God wants you to keep searching for him so he can reveal himself to you.

Keep asking and keep knocking and keep looking until you meet him at Heaven's door.

As I travel to various places I see the standards of young people's behaviour deteriorating. I notice bad language, over indulging in alcohol. I notice them binge drinking and dressing provocatively causing sexual harassment from the opposite sex.

I notice them having not many or any moral standards. I hear of men and women soliciting on the internet for sexual partners leaving families broken.

Society seems to becoming depraved and the more technologically advanced it becomes the more immoral it does also.

People do not seem to have any direction in life and you see looks of despair on their faces.

Every morning I wake-up and say a small prayer.

'Lord God in my daily life I may forget you. I pray from the bottom of my soul that you never forget me. Amen'

The signs of revelation seem to be looming ever so close. There seems to be more unrest and upheaval in the world today. We see pictures on the television of children starving and suffering because of conflicts and wars. Countries stockpiling arms that costs billions of pounds and yet poverty and hunger still exist.

Governments and leaders strive to gain power to suppress their people. Many times only one man has dictated to millions of people, keeping them suppressed and vulnerable.
The World seems to have its priorities wrong.
I want to warn these people that God knows who you are.

Governments need to stop misleading the masses and they need to be more accountable to the people they represent.

Remember the truth shall make you free.

Power hungry people with their own hidden agendas will be the first on the Hit list of God when the wakeup call comes.

God will not spare his wrath on the ungodly.

Don't Wait for the Wake-up Call

Laughter

Laughter floating through the air
Screams and giggles everywhere
Children playing all around
Oblivious to life's ups and downs
The pitter and patter of tiny feet
Racing up and down the street
Playing football, Cricket too
Doing things that children do
Living life to the full
For them a moment's never dull
No tomorrow just today
For them it seems the only way
Children's voices will be heard
If only for the final word
Parent's beware this cannot last
Your children grow up far too fast
treasure them everyone
Because far too fast your children's gone.

(By Thomas William Robinson)

Grim Reaper

Let the Grim Reaper knock on my door
Don't stand outside by the gate
Come on inside and open up your hood
I dare him to tell me my fate.
He's been once before but
I was not prepared
this time I know he can't win
Because death holds no fear
for my weary soul
So let the lesson begin.
The peace of eternity beckons to me
The course of my life has been run
All that I ask is you take me away
And bury me next to my son.

(By Thomas William Robinson)

Judas

How strange the reaction of people
When things aren't going their way
The anger that wells up inside them
And some of the things that they say
Our friendship can change in a moment
With only a flash of their eyes
Surrounded by turmoil and hatred
With a friend that they now despise
How secrets you treasured forever
With someone you thought you could trust
Are betrayed in a moment of madness
By someone who's tongue is unjust.
Never let their words defeat you
And don't let their tears cloud your eyes
And don't let hate be the cause of your fate
From the ashes let your soul arise.

(By Thomas William Robinson)

Always trust in the Lord.

Remember Satan wanted the same power as God and he is going into the pit on Judgement day.

People are becoming too complacent, dismissing Jesus as though he is irrelevant. He is more relevant now more than at any time in history. If the world's population followed Jesus we all would have Godly values, good standards, peace, love and joy in our hearts.

When a crime needs solving detectives and forensic scientists look for the evidence to solve the crime. People are dismissing vital "evidence" - that is God's word. It says in the Bible that people have eyes but they do not see so they need to start looking. People have ears but they do not hear so they need to start listening. People have brains and they need to start using them. Look at the Book of Revelation in the Bible – about the labour pains because the next thing is the birth, the wake-up call.

Jesus spoke!

*'I am the resurrection and the life;
whoever believes in me will live, even though
he dies and whoever lives and believes in me
shall never die.'*

(John 11:25-26)

Do you believe this?

When things go wrong in people's lives God gets blamed for pain, suffering and tragedies but God is not to blame. He is not the enemy Satan is.

When you realise that all you need is love then you should realise that all God wants is our love. What we do not get from each other is enough love. What we do not give to each other is enough love. As we get older we are getting closer to God. The wakeup call looms ever so near. This is when the famous words of the founder of the scouts movement means everything.

'Be Prepared'

NO Lies

I'm just a plain guy
Who tries to get by
I wont try to be something I'm not
The trouble with me
Is you get what you see
And I'll make do with what I have got
I've no airs or graces
or friends in high places
I really have no claim to fame
But the truth in my eyes
Will tell you no lies
And I hope your exactly the same.

(By Thomas William Robinson)

Jesus came to serve.

When You Are Down

When you're feeling down and weary
When nothing's going right
When the whole world seems against you
And you've lost the will to fight
And when you've always tried your hardest
To do the best you can
And you get this awful feeling
That nobody gives a damn
Don't look back in anger
it will only reflect
All the bad things that happen in life
It will eat you away
With a kind of decay
That will cut through your soul like a knife
So you must choose
Do you win or lose
The decision you must make today
Do you give in
Or do you try to win
The voice inside you will say
Life isn't easy, it isn't a game
The struggle continues for profit and gain
The life we are given
Is both yours and mine
Just try to live it one day at a time.

(By Thomas William Robinson)

When you are not living a Godly life you will be tossed about life like a rudderless ship drifting from one calamity to another, one relationship to another and not finding the peace, love, joy and stability in your life that God intended.

He wants the best for his master piece – YOU.

Every morning as I look in the mirror to wash my face I remember God and see His masterpiece in front of me.

He created you and you should give thanks and praise in His Holy Name.

On my travels I speak to people about Jesus. They dismiss him as being irrelevant in their lives. He has no place or they simply do not want him to have a place.

Do NOT take God for granted!

Do NOT be complacent.

Tap into his power with praise and let him empower your life with his love.

When everyone else fails you remember He will not. He will never leave you.

Have faith in the Lord your God and he will deliver.

People Judge themselves on being good by their own standards. When Jesus comes back to Earth he will judge them on His standards. When Jesus says get away from me I don't know you there will be wailing and gnashing of teeth and anger as Jesus dismisses them. He will dismiss them as He was dismissed.

He will close the door on they that judge themselves to be Godly people.

Remember what it says at the beginning of the book.

'I am the way
I am the truth
I am the life
No man comes to the Father
but through me'

What people should want is a clear direction instead of going through life aimlessly and constantly changing direction and never being completely happy with these changes.

If you decide not to give your life to Jesus then you will have to suffer the consequences. On Judgement day when you get the wakeup call you will have to go before the Supreme Judge and give an account of your life.

The consequences are eternal damnation.

Reading the word of God in the Bible and searching out his message and accepting him as your Lord and saviour will get you the pass you need to get through the gates of Heaven.

When you have troubles and need to call on God – Do you know what names to call him in times of trouble?

What is the name of the all sufficient one?

The God most High

Lord and Master

The Creator

The Lord is my shepherd

The Lord who heals

Father, forgive
The hatred which divides nation from nation,
race from race, class from class,
Father, forgive
The covetous desires of people and nations to possess what is
not their own,
Father, forgive
The greed which exploits the work of human hands
and lays waste the earth,
Father, forgive
Our envy of the welfare and happiness of others,
Father, forgive
Our indifference to the plight of the imprisoned,
the homeless and the refugee,
Father, forgive
The lust which dishonours the bodies of men,
women and children,
Father, forgive
The pride which leads us to trust in ourselves
and not in God,
Father, forgive
Be kind to one another, tender hearted,
forgiving one another as God in Christ forgave you.

(The Coventry Litany of Reconciliation © of Coventry Cathedral)

Heroes Of War

As I walk through the graveyards
I look at their names
Etched on the marbles of stone
So great was their pain
Now all that remain
is the memories as they lie alone

The ultimate sacrifice
Each of them gave
For the freedom that we have today
the young men we lost
In those terrible wars
Heroes we can never repay

Now silent the land
Where they made their last stand
Where the guns and the cannons once roared
Now all that we see
Is the farmers green fields
Where the memories of battles are stored

Don't glamourize the way they all died
And don't let their lives be in vain
Let the whole world unite
So there's no need to fight
And these wars never happen again.

(By Thomas William Robinson)

God will stop all wars when
the wake-up call comes.

Flying Through Space

We're flying through space
In eternal disgrace
On a planet we call our home
Were out of control
Like a ship on its own
On and on we keep going
Our world is destroyed
Through deeds we employed
For man's ambition and greed
Our crops they won't grow
It's pollution you know
And what's more we don't have the seed
Our minerals have gone
it didn't take long
for mankind to waste them away

Our future looks bleak
We have no food to eat
What we had we just wasted away
In a last desperate plea
We turned to the sea
To feed all the nations as one
Now we have nothing at all
No fish big or small
And we still don't know
where we went wrong
They say out in space
There must be a place
For a God we don't even know
This message is sent
With a cry for your help
God - SOS
Save Our Souls.

(By Thomas William Robinson)

Enter this door,
As if the floor within were gold,
And every wall,
Of jewels all,
Of wealth untold;
As if a choir
In robes of fire
We're singing here.
Nor shout
Nor rush
But Hush...
For God is here.

(Unknown)

Sin is another area people do not understand. When people keep sinning, the sins have to be paid for, so if the sons follow the sins of the father, then their curse comes on them to the 4th generation. They are passed down to the descendants of the sinner, up to 4 generations. They are passed down just like a person's genes are passed down through the mother and the father.

Look at the person of Jesus. He was without sin but he loved us so much that he took all of our sins upon himself and died for us. The devil is in the world today just looking for people to come upon to convert into sinners. Resist him with all the power of Jesus. Bind him up in the name of Jesus through his precious blood and cast him out. This is the power of Jesus when you believe in him. When you do this Satan will flee from you. Do not let Satan claim what belongs to Jesus.

Shout the name of Jesus
Praise his Holy name
Sing for Jesus
Clap your hands for him
Jump for joy
Rejoice in your heart for your redeemer
Do this in faith and Lucifer will flee from you
Just as God cannot look upon sin
Lucifer cannot look upon Godliness.

Jesus has shown you through the Bible a system of values. Through his word a way to eternal salvation so he can show you his wondrous creativity for eternity. The trouble is people want to do things their way. Remember Frank Sinatra's song *'I did it my way'* – Jesus wants you to get into his system and not your own.

To enjoy God is to see the best in him because his best is for you. He sees all the contamination of human kind such as greed, lust and envy. (The seven deadly sins are greed, lust, envy, sloth, gluttony, pride and wrath).

It has taken millions of years to put all the resources on this planet and it has taken just two hundred years to deplete it. When the wake-up call comes he is going to decontaminate us and the planet.

So it is better to clean up your act before the call comes because you won't get a chance after the call.

Are YOU ready?

Words

Words are the weapons
We use to deceive
In a world where we keep
Our foes on their knees
Where the sword is no longer
As strong as the pen
And lies are told again and again
Where truth isn't told
We can't comprehend
The meaning of words
Or how they will bend
if lies and deceit
Are the words that you speak
Then grim is the reaper
That one day you'll meet
We must learn to make do
With what we have got
Its just human nature
We must have the lot.

(By Thomas William Robinson)

Wherever Whenever Whatever

Wherever Whenever Whatever you do
Always be honest faithful and true
True to the ones that are dearest in life
Your parents, your children
your husband your wife
Faithful in marriage Whatever the cost
If you don't have each other
your future is lost
If your honest in life and in
all that you teach
You can always practice
Whatever you preach.

(By Thomas William Robinson)

Preach the word of Christ.

The other day I was reading through a magazine in a doctors' surgery. I was drawn to the problem page and I noticed how much pain, distrust and suffering there seems to be in people's lives. This need not be so. Instead of going to Agony Aunts to sort out their problems they should turn to Jesus and submit all their problems to him. They need to put their faith in him and he will bring peace, love and joy into their lives. While I was reading I came across an article on fortune telling and star predictions in which they were claiming to predict the future. God knows the plan he has for your life so instead of trying to look into your future you need to submit your life over to God and He will let you know about eternal love, peace and happiness. He knows the beginning and the end so you don't need to know what's in the future. Leave it up to God your creator.

If you focus on the love of Jesus Christ
He mends broken hearts
He mends broken lives

If you focus your thoughts on your redeemer
He takes away all your problems.

When you continue to focus on Jesus your
problems will seem insignificant.

Jesus loved us so much that he died for us.

Look at it like this.

The evidence shows us that

1. If you are married and neglect to look after
   each other the marriage breaks down and
   you part company.
You get the **wake-up call** when it is too late!

2. If you neglect your business it goes bankrupt
   and it fails through neglect.
You get the **wake-up call** when it is too late!

3. If you fail to maintain your car then it will
   break down.
You get the **wake-up call** when it is too late!

4. If you fail to look after your children they get

taken into care by social services.
You get the **wake-up call** when it is too late!

5. If you do not pay your taxes you will get taken to court and have to pay more.
You get the **wake-up call** when it is too late!

6. If you over indulge in bad morals. You are tossed about from one calamity to another.
You get the **wake-up call** when it is too late!

I could go on and on about different situations that involve a wake-up call but I am sure you get the message.

The message God wants you to get is to turn to him before you get the **wake-up call**.

Give your life over to Jesus.

Let God prompt you in the direction that you need to travel.

Step out in Faith.

Your life is like a jigsaw. When pieces are missing you become a puzzle.

Jesus wants you to find the pieces that are missing from your life. He wants to put the pieces back together and complete the picture of your life.

Love Peace Joy

I am what I am or I will be what I will be. God can keep springing surprises in history.

He wants your commitment, without commitment to the process of becoming a Christian, there can be no reality of knowing Christ.
Do you know Him?

Some people try to distort the reality of Christ. Your overwhelming desire should be to find God.

Religion is not about options to make life as you like it or pleasing to you. It is about honouring God. To love, serve and obey Him. Do this and He will give you the desires of your heart.

The trouble today is people limit God's power. They do not move forwards in faith which limits God's power. God's power was limited through unbelief. When the Israelites crossed the Red Sea through unbelief God kept them in the wilderness for 40 years.

If they had faith they would only have had to travel 11 days to get to the promised land. If people would have faith, God's power is limitless but you have to tap into this power through accepting Jesus as your saviour. Sometimes people come to Jesus and in the beginning of their faith they are hot for Jesus. Unfortunately they cool off and fall away. You have to keep looking for Jesus. To continue enthusiastically until the day you die or He returns. Never give up for He Never gives up on you. You must look for God now because you don't know how long you will have the opportunity to seek Him. We are living in what seems like the end of the present system. All the signs are starting to appear together and God is the sole possessor of all our tomorrows'.

"O God, who's longing is to reconcile the whole universe inside your love. Pour out your abundant mercy on your church and your world. So fragmented and torn apart; this we plead through the love of Jesus Christ which already surrounds us".

(Source unknown)

I believe the countdown started with the rebirth of Israel in 1948. This date marked the beginning of the countdown for the end of time of the present system. This is when the countdown started for the wakeup call.

We may never pass this way again. There is no guarantee that we will be here tomorrow so the best time to accept Jesus as your saviour is now. Seek him while there is still time. We live in all kinds of insecurities but God gives security in you heart as well as peace, love and joy.

Do you know that God said

'Let there be light'?

Do you know that God created Heaven and Earth and all the planets including the sun and moon?

Do you know that God created Nature with all the trees, birds and bees?

God created every living creature.

Do you know that God created you while you were in your mothers womb and He knows every hair on your head?

Do you know why you were created?

Do you know the God that parted the waters at the Red Sea to get his chosen people to safety?

Do you know the God that gave Moses the Ten Commandments. The standards we all should live by?

One of our greatest statesmen said *'ninety-eight percent of people stumble across the truth from time to time but quickly get up and dust themselves off and move on as if nothing had happened'*.

REMEMBER these WORDS

Never will I leave you

Never will I forget you

Never will I forsake you

God is waiting right up to the wake-up call. You need to search him out for your eternal salvation. Do not forsake Him.

Keep knocking

Keep asking

Keep seeking

We need to take responsibility and seek God and to tap into His power that will change our circumstances.

It is better to look God over than to overlook Him as you don't want to spend an eternity in Hell.

When I discuss Jesus unbelievers try to distort, change, manipulate or belittle God's word, works and deeds to justify their own unbelief. Do not be misled into untruths.

Christianity is the fastest growing religion in the world today and it is increasing more and more. We are entering a period where Revelation in The Bible seems to point to apocalyptic times ahead as all the tribulation in the World seems to be appearing more frequently.

Newspapers and magazines tell of pain and suffering with Agony Aunts trying to solve people's problems. Newspapers are also to blame for bringing morals down by showing nude girls on front pages of newspapers and magazines. They seem to highlight sexuality to sell papers with naked women advertising all sorts of immoral acts.

The television is also responsible as they show images. There are marriage breakdowns leading to divorce. Society is lacking in morals and standards that we all need to live by and those standards are getting lower and lower.

Young people of today are being bombarded with images of a sexual nature both on the television and in music videos. No wonder there are so many sexual diseases. Abortion rates have risen due to promiscuity. All we seem to read about today are the immoral acts of famous celebrities and other influential people who really should be setting the standards for the youth of today.

It is no wonder that the young people of today seem to lack direction and are being misled by the ungodly.

An unborn child's Cry

Mammy what they're doing to me
They're pulling me apart
First my legs
Now my arms
Don't let them take my heart.

My mammy didn't want me
She caused a lot of pain
I was left to die unborn
Like a kitten in the rain.

They're hurting me so hard
They're pulling bit by bit
Why can't I see the world today
It can't be that bad can it.

Well now I've nearly gone
So I'll have to say goodbye
I hope someday I'll come back
To laugh and love and cry.

(Sheila Robinson – Perangie 01/05/85)

The Countdown for the wake-up call
has already begun.
I urge you to look as all the signs of Revelation
are starting to appear more frequently together
and 80% of all the prophecies have already been
fulfilled.

Draw nigh to God and He will draw
nigh to you.

(James 4:8)

Don't be a reject when the wake-up call comes.
Don't let Satan condemn you
into eternal damnation.
Ignorance of the law is no excuse.
Ignorance of God is no excuse.
Seek Him while He can be found.

God so loved the world that He gave His only
begotten son. That whoever believes in Him
shall not perish but
have eternal life.

(John 3:16)

Believe in the Lord Jesus Christ and thou shall
be saved and thy house.

(Acts 16:31)

The heart of living is the art of knowing
how to believe in God for
Eternal salvation.

Faith

For my thoughts are not your thoughts, neither are your ways my ways.

(Isaiah 55:8)

There are a lot of people who have chosen not to give their lives out to Jesus.

They have rejected salvation.

There are lots of people who choose to sit on the fence. They have already chosen by not committing their lives to Jesus. There are lots of people who think they are saved but are ungodly. The only way through Heaven's gates is by knowing your redeemer Jesus Christ.

Do you know your redeemer Jesus Christ?

If you are for Christ and have accepted Him as your saviour you will live for eternity in the house of the Lord.

If you reject him you are Anti-Christ and you are condemned to eternal damnation with Lucifer.

What does it profit a man if he were to gain the whole world and suffer the loss of his soul?

(Mark 8:36)

For by grace are ye saved through faith and that not of yourselves. It is the gift of God.

(Ephesians 2:8)

Blessed are those who have seen and believed, but more blessed are those who have not seen and believed.

(These words were spoken by Jesus to His disciples.)

Behold I stand at the door and knock. If any man hears my voice and opens the door I will come into him and will dine with him and he with Me.

To him who overcomes I will grant to sit with me on my throne as I also overcame and sat down with my Father on His throne.

(Revelation 3:21)

One Of Gods Creations

On a cloudless night
When a full moon glows
When the shadows fall
And a cold wind blows
Across the meadows stony ground
Flies the wise old owl on its nightly round
A creature who has so much grace
With a halo that surrounds his face
As he stands upon his favourite post
A silhouette of an earthly ghost
Beauty there for all to see
As long as he is flying free.

(By Thomas William Robinson)

No Matter What

No matter what happens
It still marches on
No one can get in it's way,
No one can buy it
It isn't for sale
It marches by night
And it marches by day.
No one can own it
Or say it is theirs
There isn't a price you could pay,
It only goes forward
It has no reverse
And no one changes its way.
The older we get
The faster it goes
Where it goes to nobody knows,
I truly could say I wish it was mine
What I refer to is what they call time.

(By Thomas William Robinson)

1. Blessed are the poor in spirit for theirs is the kingdom of Heaven.
2. Blessed are those who mourn for they shall be comforted.
3. Blessed are the meek for they shall inherit the Earth.
4. Blessed are those who hunger and thirst for righteousness for they shall be filled.
5. Blessed are the merciful for they shall obtain mercy.
6. Blessed are the pure if heart for they shall see God.
7. Blessed are the peace makers for they shall be called sons of God.
8. Blessed are those who are persecuted for righteousness sake for theirs is the Kingdom of Heaven.
9. Blessed are you when they revile and persecute you and say all kinds of evil against you, falsely for my sake.
10. Rejoice and be exceedingly glad for great is your reward in Heaven for so they persecuted the prophets who were before you.

(Beautitudes –Mathew)

Rejoice for great is your reward in Heaven.

But the meek shall inherit the Earth and shall
delight themselves in the abundance of peace.

(Psalms 37:11)

Neither has the eye seen nor the ear heard, nor
has it entered into the hearts of man what God
has in store for those who love Him.

(1 Corinthians 2:9)

Enter ye in at the strait gate for wide is the gate and broad is the way that leadeth to destruction and many there be which go through because straight is the gate and narrow is the way which leadeth unto life and few there be that find it.

(Mathew 7:13 – 14)

And God shall wipe away all the tears from their eyes: and there shall be no more death, neither sorrow nor crying, neither shall there be any more pain: for the former things are passed away.

(Revelation 21:4)

We Need You!!!

This is how Jesus told his disciples to pray:

<u>The Lord's Prayer</u>

Our Father, who art in heaven,
hallowed be thy name.
Thy Kingdom come,
thy will be done,
on earth as it is in heaven
Give us this day our daily bread.
And forgive us our trespasses,
as we forgive those who
trespass against us.
And lead us not into temptation,
but deliver us from evil.
For thine is the kingdom,
the power and the glory,
for ever and ever
Amen.

When you commit your life to Jesus Christ and accept Him as your saviour there will be a change in you. Just as the baby Jesus grew, Jesus will grow in your heart and your inner being will change.

PRAISE GOD.

Christ has told us that He will arrive like a thief in the night.

<u>The Wake-up Call</u>

For the Lord Himself will descend from Heaven with a shout, with the voice of the Archangel, and with the trumpet of God: and the dead in Christ will rise first: then we who are alive and remain shall be caught up together with them in the clouds, to meet the Lord in the air: and thus we shall always be with the Lord:

(1 Thessalonians 4:16 – 17)

The middle East is the powder Keg, due to all the hostility and animosity towards Israel and God's chosen people.

Israel is surrounded by hostile forces trying to
destroy it.
God won't allow this to happen.
Keep alert for the Anti-Christ!
Keep watching events all over the world as well
as Israel and the Middle East.

To say there is no Jesus is to deceive yourselves.
The only way to escape hell is to
accept Jesus Christ.
He took the sins of the world upon himself.
He made the ultimate sacrifice for us.
Go down on your knees and
give thanks to him.

This is what Jesus wants for you:

Psalm 23

The LORD is my shepherd; I shall not want.
He maketh me to lie down in green pastures: He
leadeth me beside the still waters.
He restoreth my soul: he leadeth me in the paths of
righteousness for his name's sake.
Yea, though I walk through the valley of the
shadow of death, I will fear no evil: for thou art
with me; thy rod and thy staff they comfort me.
Thou preparest a table before me in the presence of
mine enemies: thou anointest my head with oil; my
cup runneth over.
Surely goodness and mercy shall follow me all the
days of my life: and I will dwell in the house of the
LORD forever.

If you decide to journey towards your creator
and seek Him out – I want you to know:

'A journey of 1000 miles begins with one step'.

(Ancient Chinese proverb)

So I urge you to step out in faith.

Seek and you will find.

Knock and the door will be opened.

If you study law you could become a solicitor or a barrister. If you study medicine you could become a doctor or surgeon. If you marry you will get to know that person rather than another. You will know that person and be affected by him/her.   It is the same in a relationship with Jesus.

It is impossible without a commitment to realise the reality of finding God or having a redeeming relationship with Him. It says in the Bible that when Jesus returns to Earth He will be on a cloud. People will be getting on with their lives unaware until they see Him.

What is about to happen?

JUDGEMENT DAY!

The title of this book is called
Don't wait for the wake-up call.

The reason I called it this name was if you get the wake-up call and you haven't already given your life to you redeemer Jesus Christ, then it will be too late.

I won't be late

I will be coming soon I won't be late
I'm starting to prepare the heavenly gate
As we draw close to the rapture
I'm looking for your souls to capture
The courtroom is ready
to administer my law
I hope your going through
my heavenly door
I'm the good shepherd and you should know
If you don't know my voice your going below
Repent while there's time to the God of love
Or you won't be going to the Father above.

(by James Robinson
from the Land of the Prince Bishop's)

Don't wait for the wake-up call!

The wake-up call will come when you least expect it.
If the wake-up call comes tomorrow

Do you know Jesus?

Have you accepted Him as your redeemer? Are you going to spend eternity in Heaven with God or are you going to spend eternity in Hell with Lucifer.

It's YOUR choice!

The Bible is a book of wisdom and knowledge. The word of your God. It is inspiring. Read it and you will know what God wants you to know. Pray before you open it. Pray about what you are reading. Pray when you close it. Absorb its contents and give thanks for the wisdom you have received.

Praise God.

The **Old** Testament
And
]The **New** Testament

The Old Testament is about prophecy about Jesus Christ.

Saviour of the World.

The New Testament is about fulfilment of prophecy by Jesus Christ.
Saviour of the World.

In the Old Testament Jesus is predicted.

In the Gospels Jesus is revealed.

In Acts Jesus is preached.

In the Epistles Jesus is explained.

In Revelation Jesus is anticipated.

It is all God breathed / brought into existence by the very breath of God.

Mam and Dad

Thank you Lord for my Mam and Dad
They tried to teach us good from bad
Life's so different now in so many ways
From back then what they called the golden days
Life was a struggle to meet our needs
But what they left was growing seeds
For the goodness and love that they imparted
Now grows in our hearts since they departed
I talk to them as if they were here
And many times I feel them near
The memories of so much joy and love
Could only have come from God above
My heart will always be filled with love
For my Mam and Dad
Who are in heaven above.

(by James Robinson
from the Land of the Prince Bishop's)

Focus all your attention on Jesus Christ

HAVE FAITH!
and
Don't wait for the wake-up call!

If you get the wake-up call and you have not given your life to Jesus then it will be too late and you will belong to Satan.

Jesus said:

'I am the way

I am the truth

I am the Life

No man comes to the Father

but through me'

Don't use God as your servant.
We were created to serve Him.

The Bible

It's only a moment
That gets lost in time
My body my spirit
And this life of mine

Can somebody tell me
What I need to know
Where do we come from
And where do we go

Is there somebody out there
Greater than us
Something or someone
In whom we can trust

If this is true
could I see today
A sign that forever
Will show me the way

Or must I believe
What my eyes cannot see
And believe in the words
Of a book shown to me

That book is the bible
And I have agreed
The peace that it offers
Is all that I need.

(By Thomas William Robinson)

Feast on His every word.

As pain suffering and turmoil in people's lives become more frequent, as Jesus predicts in Revelation there will be a quickening of feet going God's way as they realise that He is their only hope. Open your eyes and realise that what you are witnessing is the fall of man through greed the love of money.

Pride in oneself.
The love of possessions.
The lack of morals.
The love of power.
The lust and ungodly desires.
Being unmerciful.
Speaking lies and deceit.
Being in league with unbelievers.
Being ungodly.
Having a selfish, arrogant and sinful heart.

When God's heavenly angels, the heavenly bailiffs come to take you into God's courtroom to appear before the supreme judge how do you plead. Guilty or not guilty?

The evidence of your life is written in the book of life or death. So what will the verdict be when the wake-up call comes. What have you done for Jesus to earn redemption. Only God or you know whether you have been a good tree bearing good fruit or bad fruit.

There will be a heavenly holocaust as all unrepentant sinners all ungodly unbelievers get cast into the abyss with Satan.

I read somewhere that hearts must be pure and hands clean to anyone who dare shut the door and be alone with God.

When your expiry date is up and it is your time to go into the departure lounge, are you going through the goods to declare that means the good you have done for Jesus or are you going through the nothing to declare that means what you have done for yourself.

If you have given your life over to Jesus your final destination will be Heaven. God gave you free will to choose.

Choose wisely.

Give Him your all for He gave His all for you.

A Mother's book of Life

My life is like a book
And I'm up to chapter nine
What happened to the family
That once was mine.

You never stopped to think
When your bairns are playing on the floor
That one day very soon
They'll walk right out the door.

You want the best there is
For your daughter or your son
But you cannot pick or choose
The heart that will be won.

You try to give tips
Of how to go on in life
So they won't have what you had
The trouble and the strife.

You caught them as babies
When they stumble and fell
Who will catch them now?
No-one can tell.

Your life is half over
You've reached middle age
The book of life turning
page by page.

It's a long story
One day it will end
Then someone else takes over
The broken heart to mend.

There will be tears and laughter
And singing in the rain.
Then the pages of the book
Begin to turn again.

(Sheila Perangie – Clarey - 1990)

When judgement day comes and we get the wake up call (just as Jesus's response to revealing himself is equal to our desire to want to find him) God's judgement on sinners will be equal to the sins committed by the sinful person. In other words God's punishment will match the crimes. God's justice is fair and perfect and the wrath of God is administered to those who deserve it such as the ungodly, the people that have rejected Christ for salvation and the people who have chosen to walk in darkness with Satan.

God knows what is in your heart and your heartfelt repentance will get you into the presence of God your redeemer.

God does not choose your destiny.

You choose it yourself through free will which God gave to you.

You choose what punishment is to be administered to yourself by your ungodliness. God's judgement will give you what you deserve, nothing more and nothing less.

DONT BLAME GOD WHEN THE WAKE UP CALL COMES FOR THE DESTINY THAT YOU HAVE CHOSEN!

Eternally

When a loved one departs this life
It may be your brother,
Sister, husband or wife
It could be a friend
Or it could be a foe
It might have been different,
Were we to know
Now they are gone from life's
troubles and pain
The memories like paintings
etched on our brain
But death it can hide but it cannot divide
The Aunty, the Uncle,
The Bridegroom, the Bride.
The son, the daughter why does life end
Only through time will the pain mend
But we live on a promise
and that is you'll see
To live with the Lord Jesus Eternally.

(by James Robinson from the Land of the Prince Bishop's)

When you are down and suffering

Read 1 Peter 4: verse 12-13.

"Dear Friends do not be surprised at the painful trial you are suffering as though something strange were happening to you, but rejoice that you participate in the sufferings of Christ so that you may be overjoyed when His glory is revealed"

God's love for us

Romans: 38-39

Nothing can separate us from the love of God. "Neither life nor death nor principalities nor powers nor famine or nakedness nor height or depth can separate us from the love of Christ".

Every sin is an inside job, without holiness no man shall see the Lord.
N.B. Sin is what keeps a person away from The Bible and The Bible is a book that keeps man away from sin.

A Pentecostal pioneer called Smith Wigglesworth once said 'the best thing that could happen to you is to have a great trial in your life. It is your Robing time. It is your coming into inheritance, through trusting in God. Voice your position in God and you will be surrounded by all the resources of God in the time of your trial. He says 'Shout, Get thee behind me Satan' and you will have the best time on Earth. Whisper it and you won't. I realise this is the secret of faith in God. I now know that when the veil is lifted from your eyes and you see the answer that has been staring you in the face and God has took away your blindness and revealed himself through your experience - praise His holy name. You have moved from the darkness into
the Holy light.
I know you do not stumble across Jesus Christ by chance. He causes you to stumble so you have the opportunity to seek Him out.
Remember Jesus is the light shining in the darkness, as you move closer to the light it gets brighter and clearer to show you the direction you need to be heading.
Do not stumble about in the darkness.

I am thy God.

God said 'I am what I am'.

He will be what He will be.

He can be what He can be.

He is the way of every way.

He is the life of every life.

He is the truth of every truth.

He is the breath of every breath.

He is the being of every being.

I AM.

He will be the temper in the tempest on
judgement day.
Lord give me thy cup so I may drink of it and
claim my inheritance in thee.
Glory be to God.

I read in one of the pioneering Pentecostal books
- the essence of what
looking for Jesus is.

1. Read the word of God
2. Consume the word of God until it
   consumes you.
3. Believe the word of God.
4. Act on the word of God.

Do this and you may experience
your redeemer.

Love is the Secret

Your heart holds the secret
of God's chosen few
Whether you're in or you're out
of the Heavenly queue
If it's pure and soft and full of His love
You'll be flying towards Him
like a Heavenly dove
Don't let your heart be as hard as a stone
Or you'll never meet Jesus
in His heavenly home.

(by James Robinson
from the Land of the Prince Bishop's)

140

The Message

My heart is the receiver of
the love that God sends
Like Morse code from Heaven
I hope never ends
Now that I've found you
I can't let you go
I pray that you'll teach me
to let the world know
That the Jesus who died
On the Golgotha Hill
Is the Jesus who forgave us
and is still searching till
His flock are in Heaven and into His fold
To give us the promise as He lets it unfold
Love, peace and joy, Jesus imparts the message
from Heaven into our hearts.

(by James Robinson
from the Land of the prince Bishop's)

141

A Prayer to the Lord

Our Father in Heaven today
Hallowed your name it will be
Your kingdom will come
Your will will be done
As it is in Heaven
One day on earth it will be
Give us this day our bread as we pray
Our trespasses we pray you forgive
All the sins of others
Our friends and our brothers
I pray we'll forgive the same way
Let the tempter not tempt us
Make his evil exempt us
As you cleanse all our sins away
For the kingdom is thine
Your radiance to shine
With power and all glory divine
For ever and ever forever
Amen

(by James Robinson
from the Land of the prince Bishop's)

The Treasure

Give Him your troubles
Give Him your pain
Or in worldly anguish
He'll let you remain
Only by trust
will His glory unfold
Only by trust will you ever find gold
The treasure map in the Bible is found
Eagerly seek it and it will astound
The words you are reading
Are only God's best
And only God opens His treasure chest
but when it is opened
and God's treasure you'll see
All of this treasure is for you and for me.
Amen.

*(by James Robinson
from the Land of the prince Bishop's)*

Did you Forgive?

Lord teach us all to forgive all
So you can forgive all of us
We have to forgive to be forgiven
As we travel this life we are living
Forgive and keep on forgiving
Never give up on this task
Till one day we wake up in Heaven
That's one of the questions He'll ask
What will be the answer
We give to the Lord on that day
I pray we say we've forgiven
And pray that He'll forgive us and will say
Forgiveness and mercy I give you
I've watched you all of your days
I watched you forgive all others
And now its time to repay.

(by James Robinson
from the Land of the prince Bishop's)

One day Lord

One day Lord I'll be waiting
Waiting for your call
To take me up to Heaven
Into thy Heavenly hall
To leave this world behind me
Its troubles and its shame
Wrap your arms around me
Take away the strain
The memories left for family
To remember now and then
The good times as I grew up
To think of now and when
We embrace again at Heaven's door
And Jesus lets me see
All my little children
Now God's family.

(by James Robinson
from the Land of the prince Bishop's)

Every day do all the good you can
by all the means you can.

Every day do good in all the places you can
in every way you can.

Do good to all the people you can
every day you can as long as you live.

Let love and goodness emit from your very
being. *(this is Christ like)*

God always pays back what is due and He pays
back with lots of added interest for whatever
the interest is due.

As C. H. Spurgeon wrote,
"God is a sure pay master although He does not
pay at the end of the week".

Pay back will ALWAYS come.

I hope you have enjoyed reading this book as much as I enjoyed writing it.